understanding
**mental
health**

Autism Spectrum Disorder

Marguerite Rodger

Crabtree Publishing Company
www.crabtreebooks.com

understanding mental health

Developed and produced by Plan B Book Packagers
   www.planbbookpackagers.com
Author: Marguerite Rodger
Editorial director: Ellen Rodger
Art director: Rosie Gowsell-Pattison
Project coordinator: Kathy Middleton
Editor: Molly Aloian
Proofreader: Wendy Scavuzzo
Production coordinator and prepress
   technician: Tammy McGarr
Print coordinator: Margaret Amy Salter

Photographs:
Cover, Title page: sheff/Shutterstock.com; p. 4: yalayama/Shutterstock.com; p. 5: Pressmaster/Shutterstock.com; p. 6: -Albachiaraa-/Shutterstock.com; p. 7: Ye Liew/Shutterstock.com; p. 8: Julia Zakharova/Shutterstock.com; p. 12: Elena Rostunova/Shutterstock.com; p. 13: Doggygraph/Shutterstock.com; p. 14: Monkey Business Images/Shutterstock.com; p. 15: Suzanne Tucker/Shutterstock.com; p. 16: FooTToo/Shutterstock.com; p. 18: Kuzma/Shutterstock.com; p. 19: Kuzma/Shutterstock.com; p. 21: ollyy/Shutterstock.com; p. 22: Ioannis Pantzi/Shutterstock.com; p. 23: iQoncept/Shutterstock.com; p. 24: eurobanks/Shutterstock.com; p. 25: oliveromg/Shutterstock.com; p. 26: sonya etchison/Shutterstock.com; p. 28: somchaij/Shutterstock.com; p. 29: Albert Ziganshin/Shutterstock.com; p. 30: Daniel Loretto/Shutterstock.com; p. 32: rui vale sousa/Shutterstock.com; p. 34: Dragon Images/Shutterstock.com; p. 35: ra2studio/Shutterstock.com; p. 36: ArtFamily/Shutterstock.com; p. 37: Julia Zakharova/Shutterstock.com; p. 38: ra2studio/Shutterstock.com; p. 39: Monkey Business Images/Shutterstock.com; p. 40: mast3r/Shutterstock.com; p. 41: Pete Pahham/Shutterstock.com; p. 42: Monkey Business Images/Shutterstock.com; p. 43: Maxx-Studio/Shutterstock.com; p. 44: f9photos/Shutterstock.com; p. 45: Alex Staroseltsev/Shutterstock.com

Library and Archives Canada Cataloguing in Publication

Rodger, Marguerite, author
   Autism spectrum disorder / Marguerite Rodger.

(Understanding mental health)
Includes index.
Issued in print and electronic formats.
ISBN 978-0-7787-0081-4 (bound).--ISBN 978-0-7787-0087-6 (pbk.).--ISBN 978-1-4271-9394-0 (pdf).--ISBN 978-1-4271-9388-9 (html)

   1. Autism spectrum disorders--Juvenile literature. I. Title.

RC553.A88R64 2014   j616.85'882   C2013-907585-2
                                          C2013-907586-0

Library of Congress Cataloging-in-Publication Data

Rodger, Marguerite, author.
   Autism spectrum disorder / Marguerite Rodger.
     pages cm. -- (Understanding mental health)
   Audience: Age 10-13.
   Audience: Grades 7 to 8.
   Includes index.
   ISBN 978-0-7787-0081-4 (reinforced library binding) -- ISBN 978-0-7787-0087-6 (pbk.) -- ISBN 978-1-4271-9394-0 (electronic pdf) -- ISBN 978-1-4271-9388-9 (electronic html)
   1. Autism spectrum disorders in children--Juvenile literature.
   2. Autism spectrum disorders--Juvenile literature. I. Title.

RJ506.A9R636 2014
616.85'882--dc23
                          2013043413

Crabtree Publishing Company

www.crabtreebooks.com   1-800-387-7650

Printed in Canada/012014/BF20131120

Published in Canada
Crabtree Publishing
616 Welland Ave.
St. Catharines, ON
L2M 5V6

Published in the United States
Crabtree Publishing
PMB 59051
350 Fifth Avenue, 59th Floor
New York, New York 10118

Published in the United Kingdom
Crabtree Publishing
Maritime House
Basin Road North, Hove
BN41 1WR

Published in Australia
Crabtree Publishing
3 Charles Street
Coburg North
VIC, 3058

CONTENTS

Autism Spectrum Disorder (ASD) is a disorder that effects a person's brain development and makes social interaction and communication difficult.

On the Spectrum

"I was diagnosed with Asperger syndrome when I was 12. My mom was reading an article in the newspaper about Asperger, and the signs and symptoms reminded her of me so much that she took me to the doctor to ask about getting a diagnosis. At the time, my mom was looking for some explanation as to why I was doing so badly in school. Even though I can do the work, I'd have a lot of frustration fits, and I was getting picked on all the time.

That article changed things. In it, there was a list of traits that people with Asperger syndrome have. It described people with "obsessions" and who move awkwardly in their bodies. I love trains and zombies, hate sports, and I have a hard time talking to kids my age. The article made my life make sense. All of the things that were "different" about me were explained. It wasn't just that I was "weird" (like the kids at school thought). There was a reason I'm so different: I have an ASD. After diagnosis, things changed at school too. Now I do my work on an iPad, which really helps, because my writing is messy and it takes me forever to take notes. I know it sounds like small changes, but little things like that have made my life easier."
— Alex, 17.

5

A Wide Range

Autism Spectrum Disorder (ASD) is a group of disorders that affect brain development. The disabilities in this group are called syndromes. They include Asperger syndrome (AS) and autistic disorder, among others. The word "syndrome" means "run together" in the Greek language. In all ASDs, a specific set of symptoms tend to run together, or exist at the same time. These symptoms include:

- impairment in social interaction and communication

- restricted interests and imagination

- repetitive behaviors or movements

Though it's not understood exactly why these symptoms seem to occur together in people with ASDs, one thing we know for sure is that they always become apparent before the age of three—although they are sometimes not diagnosed until later. The word "spectrum" is used because people with ASDs can have a wide range of **intellectual** abilities. In fact, about 40 percent of people with ASDs have average or above-average intellectual ability. On the other end of the spectrum, about 25 percent of people with ASDs are unable to speak, though they can learn how to communicate in other ways.

A spectrum is a range used for classification. Some people with ASDs have severe impairments or developmental delays, and others have minor ones.

Understanding Mental Health

ASD, like other **neurobiological disorders**, is often misunderstood, and even feared. Little is known about the causes and cures, so people often make assumptions and harsh judgments. **Discrimination**, or judging someone based on one trait, and **stigma** are common. What we do know is that ASD affects 1 in 88 children, and that it is the fastest-growing serious developmental disability in North America. We know that it has a lot to do with the way the brain develops, but that there is nothing a person can do, or not do, to cause it. There is no "cure" for ASD, but there are many options for treatment. People living with ASDs, along with their friends and family members, face many challenges, but education, intervention, and understanding can pave the way for a better quality of life.

Every individual who has an ASD is unique, even if the disorder has characteristic behaviors.

8

Chapter 1
What Is ASD?

ASD has earned a reputation from films and books that depict freakishly gifted people who dress weird and have no idea how to communicate with others. If you relied on popular culture to tell you about ASD, you would think everyone who has an ASD is super smart and super weird. The thing is, describing ASD is like describing the color purple—there are dozens of shades, and each one is different.

Researchers have learned a lot about ASD since it was first identified in the 1940s. Every day, researchers are making new discoveries and coming up with new treatments. ASD is fascinating and complex, but learning about the disorders that fall along the spectrum can provide a lot of insight into the people who are affected by autism.

What Are the Disorders?

No two cases of ASD are exactly the same. The word spectrum says it all: people with ASDs may all have a specific set of symptoms in common but, in each case, the severity of the symptoms can vary. Research is beginning to uncover different areas of the brain that are affected by ASD. Symptoms and behaviors depend a lot on the areas of the brain that are affected, and how severely they are affected.

ASD Characteristics—The Basics

Autistic Disorder

From a young age (36 months or less), children with autism interact less with the world around them than other children their age. For example, they may not make eye contact with their parent(s), and they may not babble the way other babies do. Additionally, they may not smile, or show other feelings through their facial expressions. They also may not respond to their names when someone calls to them. Children with autism also show repetitive behaviors, such as rocking back and forth or twirling around.

Autistic disorder is sometimes accompanied by an intellectual disability, which affects the ability to learn and use information. Many children with autism don't speak. Some children with autism disorder learn to speak later than other children their age do. When they do begin to use language, they may not use it for conversation. Instead, they may echo words that others say, or repeat certain words over and over.

People with an autistic disorder can also experience sensory sensitivity, meaning that their senses of sight, sound, touch, taste, and smell can be heightened, and extremely sensitive. This can make everyday situations overwhelming.

Asperger Syndrome

Children who show autistic behaviors (such as difficulty socializing and repetitive movements), but who have good language skills, are often diagnosed with Asperger syndrome. People with Asperger syndrome have average or above-average intelligence. In fact, they often have the ability to learn tons of facts about their favorite subjects.

PDD-NOS

Pervasive Developmental Disorder Not Otherwise Specified (PDD-NOS) is a developmental disability that shares some of the same characteristics as autistic disorder, but not all. For example, children or adolescents with PDD-NOS might be unable to communicate and socialize, but they may not show repetitive movements such as rocking or twirling. In other words, PDD-NOS is a form of autism in which some of the symptoms are present, but not all.

Childhood Disintegrative Disorder

Childhood Disintegrative Disorder (CDD) is an ASD that has the same symptoms and characteristics as autism disorder, except that the symptoms set in after the age of three. For example, a toddler may be toilet trained, speaking in full sentences, and interacting with their parents, but then lose these skills after the age of three, and all within a few months.

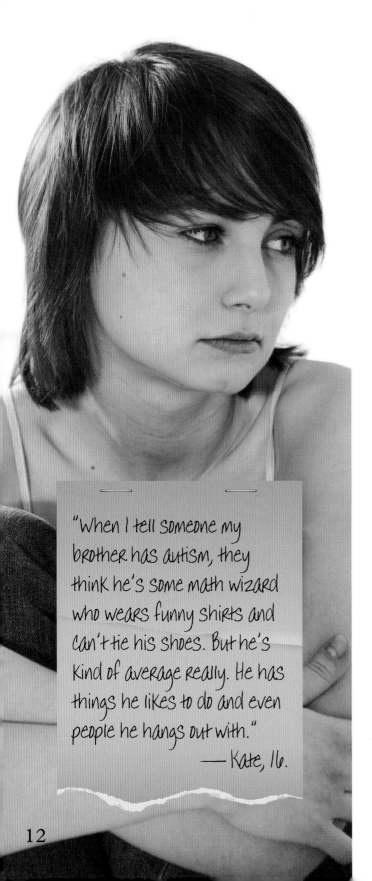

"When I tell someone my brother has autism, they think he's some math wizard who wears funny shirts and can't tie his shoes. But he's kind of average really. He has things he likes to do and even people he hangs out with."

— Kate, 16.

Feels Like This...

The main thing to remember is that the signs and symptoms of ASD can vary from person to person. But most people with ASDs, whether they can say so or not, will tell you that anxiety is a big part of how it feels to be autistic.

Anxiety is intense and overwhelming feelings of fear and panic. With that feeling of panic, comes frustration. The frustration might come from hearing irritating noises (or being overly sensitive to these noises) or having too many people around. Or it might come from wanting to communicate but not knowing how because it involves interacting. To interact effectively, a person needs to learn signs, signals, and unwritten rules. Built-up frustration often results in meltdowns or sudden freak outs.

What Causes ASD?

There are a few different theories on what causes ASD, but none have been proven so far. Just as there are many different forms of ASD, there may be many different causes.

The debate over whether ASD is inherited is an important and complicated issue. Researchers seem to agree that **genetics** do play a role in ASD. Children with a sibling or a parent with an ASD are more likely to have it themselves. Additionally, people with other genetic and **chromosomal disorders** such as Down syndrome may be more likely to have ASDs. Brain scans have shown that people with ASDs have a different brain shape and structure than people without ASDs. Researchers think this may be caused by certain genes, but they haven't been able to pinpoint exactly which ones. More likely, it is a combination of genetics and other environmental factors that cause ASD.

We don't know exactly what causes ASD. Research shows brain structure may have something to do with it.

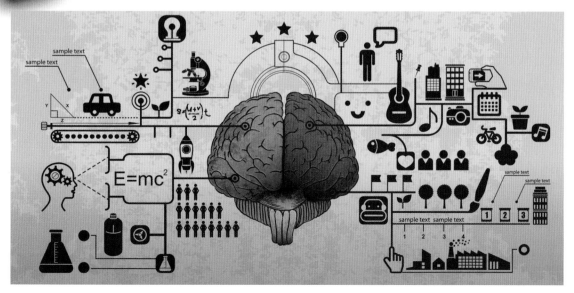

Other Research

Some research suggests that there may be other factors causing the onset of ASD, specifically ones that affect the development of babies before they're even born. There are many, many things—from stress to environmental pollutants to medications—that researchers think may "activate" certain genes in pregnant women that cause ASD.

While there has been some controversy about a suspected link between vaccines and autism, there is no **scientific evidence** that vaccinations, such the measles-mumps-rubella immunization, cause ASD. Children usually get these vaccinations around 12–15 months of age. It is also around this age that the symptoms present themselves in about 40 percent of children with autism. Many scientists agree that the timing is nothing but a coincidence.

Researchers believe ASD is hereditary for some people.

Not Alone

ASD affects people of all races, **ethnicities**, and **socioeconomic groups**. According to the U.S. Centers for Disease Control and Prevention, boys are four to five times more likely to have an ASD than girls. ASD affects over 2 million people in the United States alone. There is a huge increase in the number of people diagnosed every year with ASDs, while nobody knows exactly why, it's been suggested that doctors are simply getting better at identifying and diagnosing ASD. This is great news because, though there is no "cure" for ASD, there are many highly effective treatments and programs, and early and proper diagnosis is the first step in the right direction.

Boys are far more likely than girls to have an ASD.

Diagnosis and treatment are like a winding road. Sometimes it takes a while to get where you need to be.

Chapter 2

Diagnosis and Treatment

ASD is a lifelong disorder that, in most cases, can be identified early. It is usually professionally identified and diagnosed by a doctor, such as a **pediatrician**, **psychologist** or **psychiatrist**. Diagnosis is very important: without it, someone with an ASD can be easily misunderstood. Parents, teachers, and peers might mistakenly think that a child or adolescent is choosing not to participate in activities, or is deliberately acting out, when really they're displaying symptoms of ASD. A diagnosis is not only crucial for understanding an individual with an ASD, but also for planning. From education needs, to early interventions and **therapies**, a diagnosis can help put someone with an ASD on the path of treatment that suits them best. So, diagnosis is just the first step. Treatment is a lifelong process.

Seeing Symptoms

Most often, ASD is diagnosed early. Occasionally, people with ASDs who are higher functioning may not be diagnosed until later in life. This happens when ASD behaviors are dismissed as "personality quirks" and they don't significantly impair a person's ability in school and work environments. Early diagnosis of ASD usually happens when parents notice that their child has particular behaviors, or if they suspect that their child isn't developing at the same rate as other children their age.

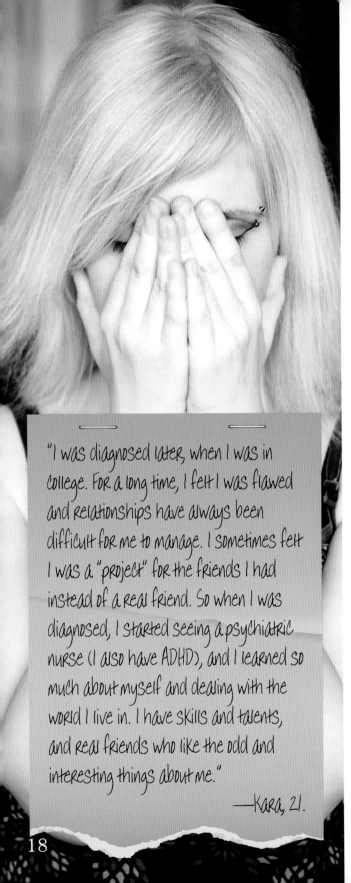

"I was diagnosed later, when I was in college. For a long time, I felt I was flawed and relationships have always been difficult for me to manage. I sometimes felt I was a "project" for the friends I had instead of a real friend. So when I was diagnosed, I started seeing a psychiatric nurse (I also have ADHD), and I learned so much about myself and dealing with the world I live in. I have skills and talents, and real friends who like the odd and interesting things about me."

—Kara, 21.

Is There a Test?

Since researchers haven't yet concluded that a specific gene causes autism, ASD cannot be identified through a blood test (or any other type of medical test, for that matter). Instead, doctors look for particular symptoms if they suspect a person might have an ASD. Some common symptoms include difficulty making friends, repetitive movements, and limited or overly intense interests.

Doctors often use a manual called the DSM (the *Diagnostic and Statistical Manual of Mental Disorders*) to help make a diagnosis. It is a textbook published by the American Psychiatric Association, which includes definitions of mental disorders such as ASD and lists all of their symptoms. It helps doctors diagnose their patients with specific disorders based on the symptoms that they have.

Treatment for ASD

Once a person is diagnosed with an ASD, there are many different choices to be made to make sure that they are getting the best treatment. Treatments and educational programs can reduce the challenges that people with ASDs face. However, there are so many types of therapies and programs that it may be hard to know where to start. Programs or medications that may work for one person may not work for another. Figuring out the best program usually involves a lot of patience, and trial and error.

Researchers know that for many children diagnosed with ASDs, early treatment, or intervention, is the key to success. Early intervention usually involves behavioral management programs that are very structured and organized. The programs use trained therapists who work one-on-one with an autistic child to help him or her develop skills and methods of communication. The programs include music therapy, medications, diet changes, behavioral training such as applied behavioral analysis, and other therapies.

Many different therapies, including music therapy, are used to help children with ASDs learn to interact.

Co-occurring Disorders

There are several co-occurring disorders that can accompany ASD. This means that, in addition to being diagnosed with an ASD, a person could also be dealing with other physical or mental disorders. The existence of these other disorders may be "red flags" that lead a doctor to a diagnosis of ASD. Common co-occurring mental illnesses conditions include obsessive-compulsive disorder (OCD), depression, and attention deficit hyperactivity disorder (ADHD). Other conditions that commonly present themselves alongside ASD include Fragile X Syndrome, dyslexia, Down syndrome, epilepsy, and many digestive issues. People with ASDs often have trouble sleeping too. Identifying as many co-occurring disorders as possible give doctors and families a better idea of what treatments may be effective. Doctors treat the symptoms of co-occurring disorders with medications and other therapies. If someone is diagnosed with an ASD, epilepsy, and an anxiety disorder, there are medications available that may help control seizures and reduce stress and anxiety. These types of medications can become a part of an effective treatment program.

Late Diagnosis

People with ASDs aren't always diagnosed as children. Sometimes, ASD can be overlooked when a person has several disabilities at once. Also, because ASD is a spectrum disorder, some children with ASD don't have symptoms that are severe or noticeable enough to cause concern. Many people who are considered high-functioning are perfectly capable of navigating their way through school and other social settings without assistance. This is particularly true of people with Asperger syndrome, due to their average or above-average intelligence.

Doctors are getting better at identifying ASD, thanks to new research. Additionally, with more websites and literature dedicated to the topic, some people may begin to suspect that they fall somewhere in the spectrum, which can lead them to seek a doctor's professional opinion. People who may not have been diagnosed with ASDs as children can be diagnosed as teens or adults. A diagnosis later in life often sheds some light on particular quirks,

such as difficulties making friends, poor motor skills, and heightened sensitivity to sound or touch. Understanding the reasons behind such difficulties can make them much easier to bear. Diagnosis can also open the door to opportunities such as therapies that may help in managing some ASD symptoms.

Information found on the Internet has encouraged many people to get a medical diagnosis. You should never diagnose yourself.

Stigma singles a person out. It prevents people from seeing people with ASDs as individuals with unique and important skills and abilities.

Chapter 3
Dealing With Stigma

People living with ASDs and other neurobiological disorders deal with stigma all the time. They may not feel shame themselves, but other people may judge, make fun of, and fear their behaviors. This is often due to a lack of information and understanding about ASD. Stigma can have many serious and negative consequences that affect the quality of life and the well-being of the people who are stigmatized. Stigma can be countered through education and understanding.

Social stigma is an extreme disapproval of a person or group of people based on social traits or characteristics that are perceived as different or devalued. Social stigma is shown in many ways, including discrimination or negative treatment. Uninformed comments or assumptions about a person's abilities can also create social stigma. If you have an ASD and are high-functioning, stigma could prevent people from seeing your potential, which is a form of discrimination.

"It may not bother my brother what other people think of him, but it bothers me. They don't see him as a human being. To them, he is just someone who is defective—a gross freak who isn't worth being around. And what bugs me about that is even adults, parents, and some teachers, think that is okay. It's not okay to ignore and avoid someone, or think they are a burden on society because they are severely autistic. It's not okay to call them 'retard' and play tricks on them. It's not okay to forget about them. They need us. We need them to teach us to be good humans."

—Keith, 18.

Fear and Ignorance

While researchers learn more every day about mental health disorders and disabilities, there is still a lot we don't know, including the causes of some disorders. Some studies have shown that even doctors themselves don't feel prepared enough to adequately care for young people with chronic complex conditions such as ASD.

The Harm Done

Stigma can manifest in many ways and the results are traumatic. They include:

- low self-esteem, and even self-stigma

- bullying, violence, and discrimination at school or the workplace

- difficulty finding jobs and careers, housing, and (where applicable) medical coverage as adults

Many people with ASDs may appear oblivious to the outside world, but that doesn't mean they don't know what is going on. They have feelings like anyone else—they just express them differently. Some people with ASDs self-stigmatize. If they don't appear visibly disabled, they may try to hide their disorder from others. They might believe that, if people knew, they would reject them or assume they would not be capable of having meaningful relationships or doing meaningful work. It's impossible to assume what a person with an ASD is capable or incapable of, based on their diagnosis alone. Stigma can also happen with family members who are embarrassed or ashamed of their sibling or child having an ASD. They may try to ignore the diagnosis, or place blame for it.

Stigma harms family members as well, as they are often forced to explain or stick up for their loved ones who are stigmatized.

25

Undoing the Harm

Dealing with stigma can be a frightening and confusing experience. Some people with ASDs deal with stigma from a very early age, before they are even able to understand the reasons for such discrimination or the effects it can have on them. Whether it's being bullied for being different or being left out of activities at school or at work, stigma not only harms children and adults with ASDs, but it harms their families too.

From hand flapping and shouting to having tantrums and speaking too loudly, some symptoms and behaviors of people with ASDs can draw a lot of attention from others. This can be difficult for family members and friends of people with ASDs. They may feel embarrassed or frustrated. They might also want to protect their loved one from the frequent stares and whispers of strangers. Each and every feeling that comes with caring for someone with an ASD is normal and, while dealing with stigma may be a daily occurrence, there are strategies that can help counteract stigma.

Sticking It to Stigma

It's important not to let the fear of stigma overshadow your efforts to fight it. You can self-advocate if you have an ASD, or understand and support people with ASDs if you are a caregiver. If you have, or someone you know has an ASD, here are some tips for fighting back:

- **Talk it out:** Talking about stigma is the best way to eliminate it. Talk to your teachers and friends about ASD, and let them know that it's not something to be afraid of, or to make fun of. The more you talk, the more people will learn.

- **Be assertive:** Don't be afraid to speak up. When people stare and whisper, it can be extremely frustrating. Address the negative attention. If you find that people are staring, don't react with anger. Speak to onlookers in an honest straightforward way. Calmly say something such as, "My brother has autism, and he's a little frustrated right now. Would you mind giving him some space?" Using a kind voice accomplishes a lot.

- **Ask for help:** Don't let the fear of stigma keep you from seeking support.

- **Don't do it alone:** If you or someone you know has been diagnosed with an ASD, it's important to surround yourself with supportive people. Check online for local support groups, or for ASD-related chat rooms and forums where people can post messages and participate in discussions.

- **Distinguish the person from the diagnosis.** Sometimes, it becomes difficult for people to see past a person's ASD. If you have an ASD, some people prefer to say "I have an ASD," instead of "I am autistic." This can let people know that you are an individual first, and that your diagnosis is just a part of who you are.

ASD is a puzzle. Finding ways to deal with behavior is like finding a piece of the puzzle.

Chapter 4
Managing Behavior

Living with ASD means living with the array of symptoms and behaviors that accompany the disorder. Many of the behaviors that people with ASDs exhibit are a sign of something deeper: **stereotyped** behaviors such as rocking and hand flapping can be a sign of stress or sensory overload, while tantrums or self-injury can signal frustration, anxiety, or fear. Learning to manage behaviors such as these is an important part of any therapy program. Understanding the causes for such behaviors is the first step in learning to effectively manage them.

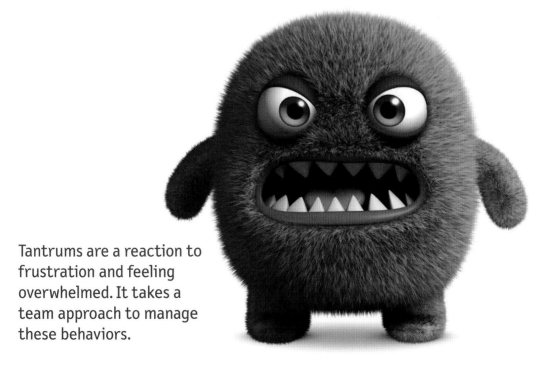

Tantrums are a reaction to frustration and feeling overwhelmed. It takes a team approach to manage these behaviors.

Freak-out or Frustration?

There are some trademark behaviors that are symptoms of ASD. These include repetitive routines or movements such as flapping hands or arms, body rocking, and constant humming. These behaviors are sometimes called "stimming," which is short for self-stimulation. Similarly, tantrums and self-injury—two behaviors that frequently present themselves in young people with ASDs—can appear to happen for no reason or out of the blue. While the reasons for these behaviors are not always apparent, they are all coping mechanisms and they may be an attempt to deal with feelings and situations that are overwhelming. Many people with ASDs cannot express their feelings and needs in words. So through their behaviors, they may not only be trying to cope, they may be trying to communicate.

Lightning bolts don't usually happen out of the blue. They come with storms. Likewise, repetitive routines have an underlying reason—they are coping mechanisms.

Get Inside the ASD Head

It's important to look beyond behaviors. For a person who does not have an ASD, that means understanding what may cause an outburst, tantrum, or stimming from the perspective of the person who has an ASD. Here are some examples:

- **Frustration:** I am frustrated because my dad is asking me to wear a shirt that I don't like to school today. The tag itches my skin, and it becomes hard to think about anything else! I prefer to wear my blue shirt because it is soft, and it doesn't have that strong smell of fabric softener.

- **Fear:** Today, we are supposed to go swimming, but it is raining outside. Now, my mom is telling me that we're going to the library instead. I really don't want to go to the library, I want to go swimming! My swimming bag is packed, but my bookbag is not. I'm not prepared for the library, I haven't finished reading my books!

- **Needs and wants:** The menu at my favorite restaurant has changed. They don't have my favorite dish anymore and, if I try something new, I might get sick. I don't know how to explain this to the waitress, so I'll have to wait until she guesses why I'm upset. This could take forever, and I'm starving!

Not every kid with an ASD has difficulty expressing their emotions, but a lot do. Imagine not being able to ask for something you wanted, or have your opinion heard. That would be really hard!

"I graduated high school last year and now attend college. I could not have made it this far without coping skills. My mom jokes that she learned the skills, but I learned them too. Having a daily routine makes me calm and helps me get things done."

— Avery, 18.

Active Coping

Studies have suggested that nearly half of children and youth with ASDs are taking medications to manage their behaviors. Others learn to cope through behavioral therapies or treatments, while some young people receive no help at all.

Managing behaviors requires a lot of planning. Here are two helpful tips:

• Be **proactive** in creating and following routines and schedules.

• Be aware that dealing with change is difficult. Most people with ASDs often have a very specific routine that they feel they cannot stray from. Following daily routines step by step is a helpful coping mechanism that gives reassurance.

Planning Ahead

You can help out by creating a schedule with your friend or family member who has an ASD, or even by creating one for yourself if you have an ASD. Young people who cannot read can use a visual schedule with pictures that represent the events of the day. Higher-functioning people with ASDs often find a written schedule useful. If there is a change to the schedule, let the person know in advance so they can adjust. If something new is added to the schedule, such as a trip to a new restaurant, prepare them by talking about the outing. Clarify what is going to happen, and what behaviors are acceptable in this new situation.

Identify stress:

No matter how well you plan and prepare, stress and anxiety can happen in life. Recognize the signs and symptoms of stress (whether in yourself or in someone else). Symptoms you might notice in yourself or someone else include a feeling of uneasiness or fear, or more frequent stimming actions such as hand flapping and rocking back and forth. In those who are verbal, you may notice an increase in the amount of questions asked about the situation.

Coping skills:

Redirect behavior using different tips and tricks to stifle an escalating situation. Some people find that sensory stimulation or distraction is a great tool. This means taking the focus off the stressful situation by using a distraction, such as a stress ball or toy, to calm down. Holding the object or toy while participating in a new or stressful situation can be comforting. Other times, "tuning out" may be the best option. Everything from music to video games to a favorite book can serve as a great escape from a stressful situation. Figuring out what works best might take a bit of trial and error. Knowing how to manage behavior is a powerful tool to have.

Friends and allies are important, even for people who find friendships difficult. Allies are people who will look out for you and defend you.

Chapter 5
Making Friends

Many people have an ability to understand how others are feeling just by looking at them. They use clues such as body language and facial expressions to figure out what the other person is thinking and feeling. Body language is a way that many people express their feelings without saying anything at all. For example, a classmate sitting alone, with their arms crossed and a frown on their face, is showing physical signs of unhappiness. Knowing how to decode, or interpret body language is a skill that combines non-verbal communication and empathy, or the ability to understand and share someone else's feeling. This ability is a great tool to have when it comes to making friends.

But what if you didn't have a natural ability to understand facial expressions? What if you couldn't tell that someone is scowling because they would like to be left alone, or smiling because they want to play basketball with you? People with ASDs don't always have the ability to decode facial expressions and body language. They may not understand what you are feeling unless you explain it to them. This can make it hard to relate to other people, and it can make social situations really difficult.

How do you think this person is feeling? Not everyone has the ability to interpret facial expressions.

Reading Between the Lines

Just as some people can "read" emotions when they look at someone else's facial expressions, some people can "hear" the intentions and feelings in another person's tone of voice. People with ASDs may have difficulty understanding the tone of someone's voice, particularly if that person is being **sarcastic**. Because of this, people with ASDs can feel left out if someone tells a sarcastic joke. When everyone is laughing and you're not, it's a stressful and confusing situation. You can help by explaining these types of jokes to a classmate or a friend who has an ASD. It will not only be enlightening, but it will reassure them that the laughter isn't directed at them.

People with ASDs such as Asperger syndrome are **literal** thinkers. This is why they may also have difficulty understanding sayings or **idioms** like "I'm on cloud nine!," and "Let's take a breather." This can be very frustrating and stressful, particularly when an adult or a teacher uses idioms while giving instructions to a person who has an ASD. You can help by giving clear directions. For example, instead of saying "It looks like a bomb went off in here!" explain that the area is messy and you would like their help to clean up.

Joining In

Some people with ASDs have the ability to retain a lot of information about a certain topic that interests them. When they are trying to be friendly, you might find that they talk a lot about their favorite subject. At the same time, they may have a hard time understanding their body space and volume, which means they may stand too close or speak too loudly. Don't be afraid to politely suggest that they take a step back. You can even suggest a change in topic. People with Asperger syndrome are often happy to take well-meaning advice in a social setting.

"I like to have fun and I can have friends who aren't Aspies, but I like people to understand me. It's easier to have friends who have the same interests."

—Tyler, 18.

Living with or caring for someone with an ASD requires strength that is often hidden.

Chapter 6
Family Ties

Living with, or caring for, a family member with an ASD can be challenging and unpredictable. Some people with ASDs require constant supervision and support, which is a huge and exhausting job for anyone trying to help out. People with ASDs have a hard time coping with even the smallest change in routine. Some things that may seem like small annoyances to others, such as walking through a crowded mall or that annoying music they play at fast food restaurants, can cause them to experience a sensory overload that can lead to anxiety and panic. These types of daily occurrences affect not only their lives, but the lives of all those around them.

There is a range of emotions that come with having a friend or family member with an ASD, but all of them are normal and more common than you might think. The most important thing to remember is that taking care of a friend, sibling, or parent with an ASD can be stressful, so it's important to take care of yourself, too.

"My parents spend all their time dealing with my brother. He can't speak, he has behavior issues, he has weird sleeping hours, and he won't eat a lot of the foods everyone else eats. Sometimes I think they cater to him too much. I love him, but it just gets way out of control. Nobody has time for anything else because we're always watching him and what he does and worrying about him."

—Keanna, 17.

Stressing Out

Having a family member with an ASD may cause more emotional distress than caring for someone who has a different disability. Research shows that mothers of children with autism are more likely to suffer from depression than mothers of children who have other disabilities. The rate of major depression in close relatives of children with ASDs is 37.5 percent. Acting as a caregiver for someone with an ASD is a huge task, and family members need to think about self-care. Some self-care suggestions include

1. Set aside some "me time" away from the family member who has an ASD.

2. Learn relaxation and deep breathing techniques.

3. Accept help from people.

4. Exercise can help with anxiety and frustration. Just 30 minutes of brisk walking a day can help.

Anger, Frustration, and Guilt

If you have a sibling with an ASD, you might feel resentful or angry because you have to take care of them or include them when you hang out with your friends. Similarly, it can be frustrating when you get punished for bad behavior, and your sibling with an ASD does not. Feeling resentful or angry often leads to another heavy emotion: guilt.

It is really important to be able to talk to someone you trust about the feelings you're experiencing. Talking it out means that you're not keeping everything bottled up inside. Sometimes, meeting other families and siblings of children with ASDs helps because you can share with someone who has similar views and experiences. This can be done at support groups, or through autism awareness organizations. To start connecting with people in a situation just like yours, check the "Other Resources" section at the back of this book, or contact your local autism society for advice.

Chapter 7

ASD Toolbox

Whether you've been diagnosed with an ASD yourself, or have a friend or family member with an ASD, coping with the daily realities of living in the world takes a lot of energy and effort.

It's really important to have "toolbox"—a plan of positive helpful tips and tricks you can use to help you cope with whatever stresses might come your way. ASD is a lifelong disorder, and dealing with the symptoms, behaviors, and stigma requires focused attention.

By keeping the following ideas in mind, you can learn to take the best care of yourself. Pick and choose the coping "tools" that work best for you to take good care of yourself, and benefit those around you too!

How to Deal

No matter what stresses come your way, it's really important to be gentle with yourself. If you've been diagnosed with an ASD, or have a friend or family member who has been diagnosed, recognize that dealing with school and life requires preparation and team work. Here are some tools to help a person with an ASD deal with life:

- Some people with ASDs have an item or tool that they keep with them to use for comfort when they are stressed. It can be a smooth stone or a squeeze ball that can be carried with them or kept in a backpack.

- Your school or class should have a "chill out" space where you can go when you're stressed. If you are aware that you're frustrated, tell someone and ask to remove yourself from the stressful situation.

- Have prompt cards in a school binder. These cards should list steps to take in an anxious situation, such as if you miss your bus or forget your lunch. They can also list trusted people to ask for help.

- Use organizational tools such as schedules and binders with colored sections for different courses, and folders for assignments.

Conflict at School

Despite your best efforts to manage your behaviors and take the very best care of yourself, conflicts can arise. Whether dealing with a bully, or a teacher who might not understand behaviors associated with ASD, conflict can be very stressful. If you or someone you know has an ASD, you may find that you need to advocate. This means that you may need to educate others so that they understand ASD and its symptoms. Try to do this in a calm and kind way. You can explain by telling them what ASD means, and that certain behaviors are symptoms of ASD. Hopefully, an increase in understanding will lead to a decrease in conflict.

Even if those around you understand ASD, and you feel that you are in a supportive environment, you may still feel stress. This can lead to conflict, so try to have supports in place that you can turn to when you're feeling overwhelmed. If you have an ASD and are able to identify when you are feeling stressed, develop a plan to cope. You can ask for permission to take a walk through the school halls to try to calm down, or even have a plan in place to visit one of your favorite teachers when you're stressed out. If you can diffuse a rage or a stressful situation before it gets out of control, you can save yourself a lot of distress!

Tips for a Healthy Lifestyle

A healthy lifestyle is very important for people with ASDs and their family members. Studies show that 19 percent of young people with ASDs in the U.S. are overweight, and an additional 36 percent are at risk for being overweight. Young people with ASDs may shy away from exercise because of low self-esteem and poor motor skills. But playing sports can help increase motor skills, and it's a way to learn to communicate and socialize with peers. You don't have to join the track team. Some people with ASDs enjoy swimming or hiking. Exercise is also a great way to ensure that you'll get a good night's rest. People with ASDs often have difficulty sleeping, and it's important to get a full eight hours of sleep. Tiring yourself out with some exercise can help you sleep better at night.

When Food Is a Problem

Many people with ASDs have food sensitivities and digestive issues and are more likely to have bouts of diarrhea and constipation. Many are also very particular about what they eat—eating only a few different foods. Food sensitivities and the fear of new foods sometimes hold them back from trying new foods. Junk food is tasty and easy to pick up, but it's not nutritious and can make you feel sick. Each week try choosing one new healthy food such as a fruit or vegetable.

Other Resources

There are many reliable sources of information on ASD. The best are produced by organizations that advocate for ASD research. Most of them have good websites. The Internet also offers a number of autism blogs written by and for young people.

Helpful Hotlines

The Autism Research Institute
1-866-366-3361

This is a toll-free (U.S.) English language hotline that provides information and support for parents and caregivers with questions about ASD.

Kids Help Phone
1-800-668-6868

A free, confidential, 24-hour hotline staffed by professional counselors. Supports youths who are in crisis and need help and information on a number of issues. Hotline available in Canada only. Visit their website at www.kidshelpphone.ca

Websites
The Autism Society
www.autism-society.org

America's leading grassroots autism organization, built by a community of people who advocate for ASD awareness.

Autism Speaks
www.autismspeaks.org
Autism Speaks is the world's leading autism science and advocacy organization. Their website has lots of information about ASD for families, caregivers, and teachers of people with ASDs.

The Autism Society of Canada
www.autismsocietycanada.ca
The Autism Society Canada is the largest collective voice for autism in Canada. It lists online forums, blogs, and support groups for people with Asperger syndrome.

Books

Freaks, Geeks & Asperger Syndrome: A User Guide to Adolescence, by Luke Jackson (Jessica Kingsley Publishers, 2002).
Finally, a funny honest account of what it's really like to have an ASD, written by a teen with Asperger syndrome.

Ten Things Every Child with Autism Wishes You Knew, by Ellen Notbohm (Future Horizons, 2012).
This book breaks down important facts about autism and puts them into ten easy-to-read chapters.

Apps

Model Me Kids: Going Places and Model Me Kids: Autism Emotion (free downloads from itunes.apple.com).
These free apps are specially designed for kids with ASDs. They tell social stories and teach different emotions using photos, text, narration, and music. Best of all, they're free!

Glossary

chromosomal disorders Disorders of the genes that a person is born with.

discrimination Unjust treatment of someone because of their differences

ethnicities Groups that have a common cultural or sometimes racial origin

genetics Something that is inherited from our parents

idioms Expressions that mean something other than the meanings of their individual words.

intellectual Relate to our ability to understand or reason

literal Taking words or ideas in their basic sense or understanding

neurobiological disorders Nervous system illnesses caused by genetic, metabolic, or other biological factors

pediatrician A doctor who specializes in treating children and the diseases and disorders that affect children

proactive Acting before something happens instead of after it has happened

psychiatrist A medical doctor who specializes in the diagnoses and treatment of mental illness and neurobehavioral disorders

psychologist An expert in the scientific study of the mind and human behavior

sarcastic Something said or written with irony to mock its literal meaning

scientific evidence Evidence that uses the principles and procedures of scientists to learn about the world by observing, measuring, experimenting, and testing, to find the answer to a problem

socioeconomic groups People who belong to the same income class or group, or a group's rank and standing in society

stereotyped Based on widely held but unfair or oversimplified beliefs about a type of person or a thing

stigma Shame or negative attitudes about a disorder or illness

therapies Treatments that can lessen the effects of a disorder or illness

Index